when life hands you
lemons,
make lemon-aide

the activity guide for good
mental health and recovery

a self-help book for everyone
and a curriculum for professionals

Sandy Shores BA, CSW

Illustrations by Angela Marie Shores and Charlene Noel Shores

When Life Hands You Lemons, Make Lemon-Aide
An Activity Guide For Good Mental Health and Recovery
Author Sandy Shores

ISBN: 978-0-692-11142-0

Published by
A Rockin Ruby LLC.
P.O. Box 142
Middletown, NJ 07748

This book is dedicated
to all the people who need assistance
as well as
Sean, my superhero husband,
for his love and support.

note to readers
disclaimer

The information provided in this book is designed to provide helpful information on the subjects discussed. The publisher and author are not responsible and not liable for any damages or negative consequences to any person, property, or entity, resulting from reading or following the information in this book. References are provided for informational purposes only and do not constitute endorsement of any websites or other sources. Readers should be aware that any websites or other sources listed in this book may change.

This book is sold with the understanding that the publisher is not engaged to render any type or kind of professional advice. The content of this book is the sole expression and opinion of its author, and not necessarily that of the publisher. No warranties or guarantees are expressed or implied by the publisher's choice to include any of the content in this volume. Neither the publisher nor the individual author shall be liable for any physical, psychological, mental, emotional, financial, commercial, or any other types of damages, including, but not limited to, special, incidental, consequential or other damages. Our views and rights are the same: You are responsible for your own choices, actions, and results.

This book is presented solely for educational and entertainment purposes. The author and publisher are not offering it as legal, medical, or other professional services advice. While best efforts have been used in preparing this book, the author and publisher make no representations or warranties of any kind and assume no liabilities of any kind with respect to the accuracy or completeness of the contents and specifically disclaim any implied warranties of merchantability or fitness of use for a particular purpose. Neither the author nor the publisher shall be held liable or responsible to any person or entity with respect to any loss or incidental or consequential damages caused, or alleged to have been caused, directly or indirectly, by the information or programs contained herein. No warranty may be created or extended by sales representatives or written sales materials or in any other manner. Every person is different and the advice and strategies contained herein may not be suitable for your situation. You should seek the services of a competent professional before beginning any improvement program. Any stories or its characters and entities may be fictional. Any likeness to actual persons, either living or dead, is strictly coincidental.

All the suggestions found in this book are meant in a very general way. Practical applications of these suggestions should be directed to appropriate professionals that can give sound advice pertinent to a particular individual and his or her situation.

Use of the information in this book is at your own discretion and in no way implicates the author, publisher, and their representatives accept responsibilities for how you use the information provided. All the information provided is on an "as is" basis. The publisher and author and their representatives and employees disclaim to the fullest extent permitted by law and negate all warranties, express or implied, which includes completeness, timeliness, correctness, fitness, infringement, or any particular use. You agree to hold the publisher, author, and their representatives as harmless from and against any claim, demand, or cause of action, including any legal fees arising out of claims as a result of using this website or any other material presented. This includes claims of defamation or other conduct arising out of the use of this educational material provided, including intellectual property laws, copyrights, trademarks or other trade secrets. If you do not think the above is reasonable, you are then advised not to read or use the information contained in this book.

By using this book, you agree that the author, publisher, and their representatives are free of responsibility, liability, and obligation with regards to how you use the information provided.

You agree that you will not bring any claim of responsibility against the publisher, author, its representatives, and any officers, subcontractors, or employees that participate in this book and the information found within it.

Use of any of the information in this book is at your own risk. Using any of the information found in the book is at your sole risk and you must use your own judgment with regards to the value and appropriateness of such information.

contents

preface

Back in 2001, when I first began to work with individuals in recovery, I was not provided with a curriculum to help guide my clients. In essence, I created my own material to use in my daily work. My ideas were appreciated and replicated in two treatment facilities. The populations I worked with were adolescents, adults, and seniors, so this book is adaptable to many.

My goal is to teach new communication skills, new ways of coping, and new ways of thinking to promote good mental health. This volume brings the most fundamental and useful content into one location. It's user friendly and practical. I believe it will assist you, the client, as well as the professional, and I encourage all who seek help to complete it. I also recommend that the client keep this book on hand to review if difficulties arise.

I am passionate about creating quality material that speaks to people who are suffering with mental illness, chemical addiction, or are having difficulty with relationships as they struggle to find tools they need to extricate themselves from their problematic behaviors. This book will teach helpful skills without the necessity of reading a novel. This book does not need to be used in chronological order. Skipping around may help you meet your needs.

I also know that many clinicians, from beginners to even the more seasoned therapists, struggle to find creative, concrete ways to reach their clients and to assist them on their journeys. In the event your stay at a rehabilitation program is brief, the greater the reason to focus on the activities that suit your needs. I recommend that family and friends also learn the skills in this book to assist the client in achieving wellness.

Professionals can use these activities in a private or group therapy setting. It is wise for the professionals to assist their clients in exploring potential responses from others. The skills in this book are most likely new to the client, so any change from their usual interactions may take some adjustment for all. The professionals can also assign homework to get through as many activities as possible.

Many counseling sessions are conducted verbally in an open-process style. This means that the client tells the professional what's wrong and the professional offers feedback. In this style of learning, the client will process their problems, but I am adding a visual component as I teach skills of all types. This will better assist the client in achieving wellness.

A family therapy session or a multi-family therapy session is suggested and has been done using this material. This would involve the client, the client's family, and other important people in the client's life. At this therapeutic session, everyone will complete an activity, discuss it, and then be asked to practice it at home.

This book has been generated from my own life experiences, work experiences, and education. It is my interpretation of how to achieve good mental health. I have used a Behaviorist Approach which focuses on the behavior of someone's response towards external events. I have also used a Humanistic Approach which is the belief that people are innately good and are concerned with positive growth and development.

Game changer—once you learn the skills in this book and apply them to your life, no matter what your struggles, I am confident that your life will improve for the better.

acknowledgments

I would like to thank Helena Banker, MSW, LCSW; Lynn O'Connor, MSW, LCSW; and Kurt Kubinski, CADC. They were great mentors to me and are outstanding clinicians!

part 1:
help me cope

feeling or thought

Feeling Words are words that describe your emotions. Some of theses words would include *happy*, *sad*, *frustrated*, *irritated*, *loved*, and *disappointed*. Write some *feeling words* that are relevant to your circumstances.

_____

_____

_____

_____

Expressing your feelings can create powerful results. When you do this, you'll be getting your feelings off your chest or out into the open. This will promote a feeling of satisfaction as you express yourself effectively, as well as helping the person understand you.

Here's an example of using a *feeling word*: A woman says to her boyfriend, "I am *unhappy* that you brought up my past relationships. I thought we agreed not to do this." The boyfriend responds by telling her she is wrong—but she is not wrong! No one can take away her feeling! She stays calm and doesn't let herself get triggered into an argument. In fact, as he continues trying to prove her wrong, she finds herself entertained. His attempts aren't working. She has so much power (confidence) in herself that she knows she has already won the disagreement. When he finally is done talking, he apologizes.

There's no guarantee that you'll get the response you are looking for, but at the very least you will feel good about yourself.

When you're trying to communicate or confront someone who frightens you, try to offer a compliment first and then use a positive *feeling word* to try to get your point across. For example, you might say to your boss, "I am *impressed* with your decision making ability; however, I work *well* when I follow the same routine."

Here's another example of what to say involving a scary parent. "It must be *challenging* to parent me; however, I would be *happy* to listen if we could sit down and talk."

A Thought is an idea or opinion. Thoughts aren't wrong to say but they aren't as effective as feelings. Many people use thoughts because they, themselves, feel protected from getting hurt. -Curse words, name calling, and shouting are never acceptable.

feeling or thought

Now, let's look at examples of using **Thoughts**.

Scenario: A parent says, "Your crazy stunts are stupid. What's wrong with you? You're going to get yourself killed."

Here are some potential feelings that the parent didn't express:
- I get *scared* when you do reckless things.
- I become *frustrated* when I can't keep you safe.
- I am *embarrassed* because you are a reflection of my parenting skills.
- I feel like a *failure* as a parent.

Notice that the original thought seems to lack a clear explanation of what the parent is experiencing. The parent would have been more effective if he or she had mentioned any one of the feelings listed. The parent also could have used a positive statement such as "I feel *calm* when you are safe. I *hope* you will make *wise* decisions in the future."

Scenario: Mary is at a restaurant with her brother Tom. Mary wants to order dessert, but Tom does not. Tom tries to manipulate Mary by raising his voice saying, " Why do we always have to do things your way?" Mary responds, "Okay, let's go."

Potential feelings for Mary:
- *embarrassed* that others may have witnessed what happened
- *frustrated* that she couldn't stop Tom from making a scene
- *manipulated* by Tom since he knows what bothers her

Mary could have responded by saying, "I would be *happy* to listen to your opinion about dessert. In the future, I would *like* to discuss the situation before you decide to raise your voice."

The following page has a *Feeling Words* practice sheet.

feeling words practice sheet

Complete the following exercise with *feeling words.* Positive statements are encouraged and can be beneficial. Notice that these statements start with the word *I* and not the word *You.* If you start speaking with the word *You,* the person you are talking to might feel accused or attacked before hearing the rest of your sentence. If you need help identifying your feelings, see the list of emotions following this practice sheet. In the margin, you can write someone's name if you choose.

I feel _____ when you _____
_____.

I would like you to _____in the future.

I feel _____ when you _____
_____.

I would like you to _____in the future.

I feel _____ when you _____
_____.

I would like you to _____in the future.

I feel _____ when you _____
_____.

I would like you to _____in the future.

I feel _____ when you _____
_____.

I would like you to _____in the future.

feeling word list

Mostly Positive			**Mostly Negative**		
able	accepted	adequate	abandoned	abused	afraid
admired	affectionate	aware	aggravated	alienated	alone
bighearted	brotherly	calm	annoyed	anxious	betrayed
capable	carefree	charming	bitter	bored	cautious
expressive	fair	faithful	cheapened	cold	competitive
forgiving	friendly	genuine	confused	drained	dumb
glorious	grateful	happy	embarrassed	exhausted	envious
helpful	intense	joyful	fearful	forgotten	frustrated
lovable	magical	mischievous	grumpy	hesitant	ignored
nice	optimistic	powerful	inhibited	insecure	irritated
protected	proud	quiet	jealous	lonely	manipulated
relieved	reasonable	satisfied	needy	overwhelmed	put down
secure	silly	strong	rejected	ridiculed	ridiculous
terrific	victorious	warm	stepped on	trapped	useless
whole	watchful	withdrawn	weak		

anxiety! and panic attacks!

Anxiety means to feel nervous or worried about something with an uncertain outcome.
Panic Attacks are uncontrollable fear or worry about something known or unknown.
Panic attacks can be triggered by a memory, something visual, a smell, or even a sound. The cause of your *panic* may be obvious, or it may be subtle, in which the conscious brain can not identify the source.

Perhaps your 4th grade teacher, who you thought was mean, wore a particular perfume. Years later you smell that same scent on someone else. This triggers your *panic* which could be obvious to you as you remember your teacher, or subtle as you can't remember and have no idea why you are experiencing *panic*.

Think about the people, places and things that make you *anxious*. It could be anything from an abusive partner, to spiders, to lacking self-confidence. Then list all the characteristics you find troublesome about what you chose. _____

_____

_____

_____

_____

_____

_____

Now that you have fully investigated the people, places and things that make you anxious, you may be able to explain your, once unknown, *panic attacks*. However, if an unknown *panic attack* occurs again, try to investigate why. Try to observe what's happening around you and retrace your steps leading up to the attack.

Finally, what could you do to change or alleviate negative persons, places, or things in your life. As you work through this book, see what skills you could use that would help. If you are working in a group setting or with a therapist ask for feedback and try to role-play scenarios.

fair fighting

1. Identify if your disagreement is a debate or a problem that needs resolution.

    a. Debates don't need to be won. Both parties can agree to disagree.

    b. Other problems may need to be resolved.

2. Focus on the problem you have identified.

    a. Stay on the topic.

    b. If you have difficulty staying on topic, write it down.

    c. Avoid bringing up past offences.

3. Attack the problem, not the person.

    a. Use statements that begin with the word *I*.

    b. Use words that describe your feelings, such as *respected, powerless, happy, hurt, embarrassed, concerned,* or *confused*, to name a few.

4. Listen with an open mind.

    a. Try not to predict what the other person will say.

    b. If you find yourself interrupting, write down a key word or phrase for later.

    c. Make sure you use clarifying statements. "So what I hear you saying is …"

5. Treat the other person with respect.

    a. Avoid name-calling and cursing since this will cause a new fight.

    a. Talk instead of shouting.

6. Take responsibility for your actions and wrongdoings.

    a. If you are at fault for a portion of the problem, accept responsibility for that portion.

    b. Acknowledge what you have done wrong by apologizing or make amends.

7. Try to avoid complaining.

    a. Offer a solution.

    b. Tell the other person what you would like to happen in the future.

8. Negotiate a solution.

    a. Make some compromises

    b. Possibly go separate ways.

9. Practice by role-playing. (optional)

    a. Establish a pretend argument.

    b. Use the skills above to act out a solution.

the daily challenge

You must achieve each step in order to be the best person you can be. If you miss a step, you should still strive to be your best. Don't give up just because you didn't get the proper amount of sleep or you didn't eat a healthy breakfast.

Step 1 Primary Needs:
  a. Sleeping- Some adults need 8 hours and some feel better with more.
  b. Eating healthy foods- Try to achieve a well balanced diet. Watch your sugar and caffeine intake!
  c. Staying hydrated- Make sure you don't deprive yourself of fluids when you are thirsty. Alcoholic beverages will not count!

Step 2 Secondary Need:
Exercising- I exercise three times a week and feel quite satisfied. Some people like to exercise every morning.

Step 3 Be a productive member of society:
Whether you go to school, work, or stay at home, you need to be productive. If you are a child, your function would likely be to get an education and do some chores around the house. If you are a spouse who stays home, your function may be paying bills and keeping the house clean.

Step 4 Making a List:
Always make a list of things you need to do for that day. This will focus your mind so your day is productive.

Step 5 Bump free:
You will need to be free of obstacles to get the award. For instance, if you develop the common cold or sprain your ankle you most likely will have difficulty achieving this challenge. Perhaps you are wearing makeup that causes dry eyes. Your irritated eyes will take your focus off of the important things throughout your day.

Award time— You have achieved steps 1 through 5 and are the best person you can be.
-Life is not a dress rehearsal. Try not to waste it by thinking you'll do better tomorrow.

sleep techniques

Are you having difficulty falling asleep? It could be because you have too many thoughts in your head. The following techniques may help. Find one that works for you, or try them all.

1. **Make a list**—Create a list on paper of the things you need to do or whatever is on your mind. By doing this, you will organize your thoughts and won't have to remember them for the following day.

2. **Decorate letters**—To start, choose any word or your name. Imagine the word in your mind; picture it vividly. Pretend the letters are wide, block-style, and decorate each one differently. You may want to choose a background color, and a decoration such as stripes, polka dots, butterflies, stars... Stay on each letter until it is exactly the way you want it. If it's not just right, go back and change it. This activity will help you to have one thought on your mind instead of several, allowing your mind to relax.

3. **Recite a prayer**— Recite a prayer, short poem, or phrase. If your mind drifts in the middle, go back to the beginning and start over.

4. **Massage**—Massage your forehead until you notice your arm drop. Continue this action until you can't do it anymore and then just relax.

5. **Napping**—You may need to avoid napping during the day, or increase your physical exercise, or avoid caffeine in the evening.

6. **Quality rest**— If all else fails and you are still awake, give up! A deep rest will help you the following day. You should now be focused on quality rest and no longer on sleeping.

Here are a few things to avoid:
- Avoid trying to fall asleep. Observing the act of sleep is not possible.
- Avoid watching the clock. This may make you anxious.
- Avoid counting sheep. This may also make you anxious when you realize you have reached a high number and are still awake.
- Avoid playing a song in your head. Most often the song will continuously repeat.

To order more copies visit: www.whenlifehandsyoulemonsmakelemonade.com

emotions

Part 1

Can you think of someone who impacts your life in a negative manner? Circle the negative feelings you experience.

hatred	helpless	envious	powerless	embarrassed	rejected
hurt	fearful	judged	crushed	sad	frustrated
forgotten	anxious	Other? _____			

Part 2

What are some actions you have taken, or want to take, in response to the above?

argue	defend yourself	pull away	disagree	punish self	cry
yell	run away	make jokes	physically fight	hurt yourself	
use drugs	Other? _____				

Step 3

Make a sentence using a word from part 1 and a word from part 2. For example: I feel hurt when you put me down, so I want to give you the silent treatment in return.

_____

_____

_____

Step 4

Create a positive statement out of step 3.

For example: I feel good when you encourage me, therefore, I want to do even better.

_____

_____

_____

Step 5

If you are working in a group or with a therapist practice this by role playing. If you are hesitant to share your positive sentence with the person who caused you negative feelings, try inviting this person to a counseling session.

suffering a loss

Feelings of grief and loss can occur after a loved one has died. They can also occur with a divorce or breakup. The following are 5 stages to explore:

stage 1: sadness   I can't stop crying.
When you focus on *yourself* and *your* loss, you may think the following:
1. *What will I do without her/him?*
2. *How will I fill the void I am feeling?*
3. *How will I spend my time?*
4. *Who will love me now that she/he is gone?*

stage 2: anger   Anger covers up the sadness.
It's often easier to deal with anger than to examine the feelings that came before it. If you don't uncover what's under the anger you will be stuck in stage 2. If you explore your primary feelings, the anger should subside.

stage 3: blaming   I blame the doctor.
It could, in fact, be the doctor's fault, but you still need to deal with your loss. When you are faced with a tragedy, you may want to blame someone to make the situation more bearable. Be careful not to falsely blame.

stage 4: rationalizing   At least their suffering is over.
This stage assists you with acceptance. You begin to find something positive about your loss. If your loss is over someone dying, you may think that his or her soul has gone to heaven or that their suffering has ended. If your loss is over a breakup, you may realize that you were better off without him or her.

stage 5: peace   Peace is acceptance of your loss.
The following may assist you with being at peace with your loss...
1. *I know she didn't choose to leave me.*
2. *I don't want her to look down from heaven and see me sad.*
3. *I am going to honor her memory in a positive way.*
4. *I will get through this. It's okay to move on.*

To order more copies visit: www.whenlifehandsyoulemonsmakelemonade.com

manipulating

Manipulating is when someone distorts the truth to get his or her way.

List ways in which you have been manipulated:

_____

_____

List ways in which you have manipulated others:

_____

_____

Here are some examples of manipulating. How would you feel? You may choose words from the list below or come up with your own.

1. I will give you the silent treatment. _____

2. I will overreact. _____

3. I will put you down and insult you. _____

4. I will convince you to do it my way. _____

5. I will scream until you back down, cry, or hurt yourself. _____

6. I will threaten you. _____

7. I will embarrass you._____

8. I will tell you lies. _____

word list:

Powerless, humiliated, angry, disgusted, frustrated, irritated,

scared, embarrassed, defeated, sad, depressed, vengeful, mistreated, abused, bad

To communicate effectively, free from manipulating, try to be

1. genuine (truly state what something is)

2. honest (free of deceit)

3. straightforward (uncomplicated and to the point)

4. expressive of feelings (use a word that describes your emotion)

how to conquer anger

Check any of the following actions that apply to you.

Section 1

When I get angry, I …

_____hit or throw things   _____yell

_____hurt myself   _____hurt someone else (physically or verbally)

_____have bad thoughts   _____hold my breath

_____think of revenge   _____overeat or starve myself

_____clean something   _____force others to do things my way

_____do something reckless   _____spend money

_____use the silent treatment   _____walk away

_____grit my teeth   _____throw a temper tantrum

_____create knots in my stomach   _____give myself a headache

_____use substances   _____go to bed

_____withdraw   _____cry

Other: _____

_____

_____

Section 2

Does your anger

_____last too long?

_____become too intense?

_____lead to aggression?

_____flare up easily?

_____happen frequently?

To order more copies visit: www.whenlifehandsyoulemonsmakelemonade.com

Section 3

Rank each of the following statements from 1-8.

_____You overheard someone talk about you or your family in a negative manner.

_____You are not being treated with respect.

_____You get singled out and corrected.

_____You are trying to discuss something important, and are ignored.

_____Someone constantly offers you advice that you don't want.

_____You have had a busy day and the person you live with greets you with complaints.

_____The teacher's pet gets special attention.

_____Someone comments about your weight.

how to conquer anger

Think about a time when you became angry. Was there another emotion that you experienced just prior? Anger is a secondary emotion. With that said, it's important to find the initial feeling and deal with that first. This will help you stay calm and keep your focus on the primary feeling that needs to be addressed.

On the previous worksheet, "Exploring Anger Worksheet," in *section 3* decide what the primary feeling(s) might have been. You can come up with more than one possible answer. Write your answer(s) at the end of each sentence of *section 3*.

People skip over their primary feelings and go right to anger because anger covers up their vulnerability. Let's say your friend is teaching you how to snowboard. You try so hard but keep falling. It's easier to get angry and yell at the teacher than to admit you're feeling frustrated, and embarrassed.

Use the space below to write things that make you angry. Then write the initial feeling(s) that came before anger.

_____

_____

_____

_____

_____

_____

_____

Remember, if you focus on your primary feelings, you should have an easier time managing your anger.

clarifying statements

After listening to someone speak, you say, *"So what I hear you saying is …"* and then say the same words or similar words as you understood them. Then give the other person a chance to say, *yes that's right,* or *no not exactly.*

Scenario: A child is running around at the bus stop. The parent notices pebbles and sand on the road. The parent tells the child to stop running. The child does not listen, slips, and falls. He is not hurt but is now crying.

A common response by the parent: "If you would only listen to me these things wouldn't happen." The parent brushes the dirt off of her child and says, "You're okay." however, the child is still crying. Why might the child still be crying?

A clarifying response would go like this. "I'm so sorry you fell. I know it's scary to fall and you might feel embarrassed in front of your friends. Try to be more careful and listen to directions." Now that the child's feelings are validated, and since the child wasn't physically injured, there is not much reason for continued crying.

Practice:
You miss your boyfriend who is away on vacation and are crying. Your parent says, *"He will be back. Stop acting like a baby."* This comment makes you feel misunderstood, frustrated, and angry. How could your parent have used a Clarifying Statement instead? _____

_____

_____

_____

_____

_____

_____

_____

clarifying statements practice

You have had it with your bossy sister. She chose the movie you both are seeing which made you frustrated. What kind of clarifying statement can you say to get her to stop this behavior?

_____

_____

_____

_____

Your parents won't stop lecturing you about getting your nose pierced. What clarifying statement can you say to them? _____

_____

_____

_____

You are out to dinner with your boyfriend and he is unhappy with his meal. He begins to speak loudly about it. People are starting to stare, and this makes you feel uncomfortable. To acknowledge his feelings and yours, what clarifying statement can you use? _____

_____

_____

_____

Your daughter does not want to go to bed. She complains that she is not tired and her bedtime is too early. What clarifying statement can you use to encourage cooperation?

_____

_____

_____

_____

phobias

If you are working in a group, or by yourself, make a list of phobias. They don't have to be limited to your own fears. Then decide if each phobia interferes in your daily living. Let's say you are discussing the fear of swimming in the ocean. Does this fear interrupt your life? Many people would say no, they can still go to the beach without swimming.

Use the lines below to identify your fears and whether or not they impact your life.

_____

_____

_____

_____

_____

_____

_____

_____

_____

_____

_____

_____

If your fears limit your daily living try the skill of Self-Talk

feeling powerless

Often people feel powerless over certain situations and the actions of others.
Below are some reactions to feeling powerless. Check all that apply to you.

____ I wear something provocative because I only have control over my clothes.

____ I have control over my money so I waste it on things I don't need.

____ I will stop eating to make my family worry.

____ I will hurt myself to release frustration or get attention.

____ I punch walls when I am angry. I think this will make others stop frustrating me.

____ I do drugs to escape reality.

____ I have multiple piercings and tattoos. I want to look freakish so everyone will stay away.

Engaging in poor behavior usually hurts yourself. It is not an effective way to communicate. Make a list of things that cause you to feel powerless.

_____

_____

_____

_____

_____

Brainstorm some safe alternatives to alleviate your frustration. You might want to take a walk before you punch a wall, or let someone know how frustrated you really feel. List all of your ideas.

_____

_____

_____

_____

_____

help me cope section quiz

Refer to the Appendix for quiz answers.

1. True or False: It's helpful to count sheep to fall asleep.

2. True or False: A good form of communication is to use a word that describes your feelings.

3. True or False: Anger is a primary emotion.

4. Using a clarifying statement will help in which way?

    a. Gives the person you are talking to information about you

    b. Helps you to win a disagreement

    c. Informs someone whether or not you understand them

5. Major needs include sleep, eating healthy, staying hydrated, and _____.

6. People don't usually use feeling words because they are afraid of getting _____.

7. If you have a disagreement with someone, it is important to

    a. Determine if the disagreement is a debate that doesn't need to be won

    b. Attack the other person to win

    c. Use your anger to persuade

8. Your neighbor's grandfather died. When you heard about this you said, "I'm sorry for your loss." This describes _____.

    a. Blaming

    b. Personalizing

    c. Using your feelings

9. List three things you plan to do to maintain good mental health.

    1. _____

    2. _____

    3. _____

10. If you want to communicate with someone who frightens you, like a boss or parent, it's helpful to start the conversation with a compliment and then use a *feeling word,* in a _____ way.

part 2:
thinking errors

uncovering automatic thoughts

Events by themselves have no emotional content. It is your interpretation of that event that causes your emotions. So an event, perceived as negative, will cause a negative feeling.

A. Event → B. Negative Thought → C. Negative Feeling

Here's an example:
- A. Event: My car won't start.
- B. Negative thought: *Oh no, I will be late for work. I will probably encounter serious consequences at work.*
- C. Negative feeling: Anxious, powerless, and angry

A. Event → B. Positive Thought → C. Positive Feeling

If you view the same event in a different manner it might look like this.
- A. Event: My car won't start.
- B. Positive thought: *I will call for assistance, provide proof to my job, and hope they will understand.*
- C. Positive feeling: Hopeful, smart, and calm.

Here's another example:
- A. Event: You were given extra assignments at work just before quitting time.
- B. Negative thought: *I'll be here all night. I won't be able to meet my friend.*
- C. Negative feeling: anxious, frustrated, and disappointed

Reframe the thought:
- A. Event: You were given extra assignments.
- B. Positive thought: *Maybe I'll be considered for a promotion. My friend will understand.*
- C. Positive feeling: Hopeful, capable, smart, and relaxed

uncovering automatic thoughts practice

After reading about Uncovering Automatic Thoughts try some on your own.

    A.   Event: The soccer game was cancelled due to rain.

    B.   Negative thought: *I really wanted to play tonight. Now my night is ruined.*

    C.   Negative feeling: Sad

Reframe the thought:

    A. Event: The soccer game was cancelled due to rain.

    B. Positive thought:_____

    C. Positive feeling: _____

    A. Event: I only have one friend at school.

    B. Negative thought: *No one likes me.*

    C. Negative feeling: depressed, concerned

Reframe the thought:

    A. Event: I only have one friend at school.

    B. Positive thought: _____

    C. Positive feeling: _____

    A. Event: I lost the race.

    B. Negative thought: I am not good enough.

    C. Negative feeling: depressed

    A. Event: I lost the race.

    B. Positive thought: _____

    C. Positive feeling:_____

If you change the thought, you can change the negative feeling into a positive one. Spend time practicing this skill. This technique may need to be rehearsed often so your new, positive responses become automatic.

character flaws

These characteristics can appear in all people, but they can become exaggerated in some. It's important to be aware of these flaws so you can work on making some positive changes.

1. **Low Frustration Tolerance** —This person needs instant gratification. He is unable to go through any form of discomfort for any length of time: He is impatient.

2. **Grandiosity** —This person feels inferior and covers it up by acting like a big shot.

3. **Anxiety Stricken** —This person has countless fears, often unproved. Sometimes he cannot identify the source of his anxiety.

4. **Perfectionist** — This person's goals are set too high. The perfectionist sets standards that are impossible to reach. This person may also insist that others meet his or her standards as well.

5. **The Loner** —This person prefers to be alone. Friendships are usually superficial. This person slips under the radar so others won't notice him. His behavior is usually a silent cry for help.

6. **Overly Sensitive** —This person is easily hurt and has difficulty protecting his ego. He allows hurt to fester into resentment.

7. **Impulsive** — This person acts without careful consideration. This person has a need for immediate gratification.

8. **Oppositional** —This person opposes those in authority or those who try to exert authority.

9. **Dependant** — This person relies on someone else to take charge. He is unsure of himself and his decisions. He relies on others to alleviate his anxiety.

10. **Childish Adult** — This person is an adult who wants others to dote on them as when they were a child. This person is not likely to ask others how they are doing or what's happening in their lives. This person will join in conversations but only to talk about their own experiences.

WHEN LIFE HANDS YOU LEMONS, MAKE LEMON-AIDE

character flaws exercise

After reading about common Character Flaws, can you find which flaw represents the statements below?
The Flaws to choose from are:
low frustration tolerance, grandiosity, anxiety stricken, perfectionist, loner, overly sensitive, impulsiveness, oppositional, dependent, and childish adult.

1. I think I will give my teachers at school a hard time. Who cares about the rules? I will do whatever I want. _____

2. I am never going to make a mistake again! I know I can do better. _____
_____

3. I saw the candy, wanted it, and took it. I had no money and didn't feel like running home to get so. _____

4. I am afraid of heights. If I go past the second floor I will probably have a heart attack. _____

5. Bob didn't come to my party. I am never talking to him again. _____

6. I need to escape from life and need drugs to do so. _____

7. I have the finest clothes and the best job. I also help all my friends so I am sure everyone likes me. _____

8. There is too much cigarette smoke in this dance club. You have to take me home now! _____

9. People are always telling me what to do and this gets me angry. I don't need friends and would rather be alone. _____

10. Everytime I share a personal experience, my brother seems to have the same experience and takes over the conversation. _____

1. oppositional; 2. perfectionist; 3.impulsive; 4. anxiety stricken; 5. over sensitive;

6. dependant; 7. grandiosity; 8. low frustration tolerance; 9. loner; 10. childish adult

To order more copies visit: www.whenlifehandsyoulemonsmakelemonade.com

half-empty or half-full

You have your favorite drink that fills half of your glass. Do you consider your glass to be half-full, half-empty, or exactly half?

> If you said half-full, you are an **optimist**.
> If you said exactly half, you are a **realist**.
> If you said half-empty, you are a **pessimist**.

Whatever we think about, we bring about. How can you think more positively about life events? Look at the following statements. Come up with your own statements.

1. Your best friend hasn't called you in four months.

> Optimist: We have not had any disagreements, so I believe she still values our friendship. She must be busy.
> Realist: She hasn't called me in a while.
> Pessimist: She must be angry at me or doesn't care about me anymore.

2. You are a participant in track and field. You were running a race, tripped, and almost fell.

> Optimist:_____
> Realist:_____
> Pessimist:_____

3. You scored a 90 on a test.

> Optimist:_____
> Realist:_____
> Pessimist:_____

4. You broke your arm in an auto accident.

> Optimist:_____
> Realist:_____
> Pessimist:_____

5. A flood destroyed your home.

   Optimist:_____

   Realist:_____

   Pessimist:_____

6. Your spouse left you.

   Optimist:_____

   Realist:_____

   Pessimist:_____

7. Your grandmother died.

   Optimist:_____

   Realist:_____

   Pessimist:_____

8. You were fired from your job.

   Optimist:_____

   Realist:_____

   Pessimist:_____

9. You need to have surgery.

   Optimist:_____

   Realist:_____

   Pessimist:_____

10. Your puppy chewed all of your shoes.

   Optimist:_____

   Realist:_____

   Pessimist:_____

codependency

Codependency is excessive emotional reliance on a partner, typically a partner who requires support due to an illness or addiction.

Here is a list of codependent behaviors. Can you think of a time when you engaged in any of these behaviors?

1. I do more than my fair share after help is requested.

2. I do something I really don't want to do.

3. I say yes when I really want to say no.

4. I feel good about myself because I am relieving someone else's pain.

5. I speak for someone when they are capable of speaking for themselves.

6. I solve someone else's problem.

7. I put my wants and needs aside to help someone else.

8. I try to control the lives of others when my life is out of control.

9. My partner's struggles affect my serenity.

10. I try to fix people because they are incapable of doing it themselves.

11. My partner's appearance is a reflection of me so he/she needs to dress a certain way.

12. My good feelings (of who I am) depend on being liked by others.

13. My hobbies are put aside so I can participate in your hobbies.

14. I live to make my partner happy. I don't know what makes me happy.

If you notice that you engage in these behaviors to an unhealthy level, tell yourself, *you are important,* and work towards living a healthier life.

positive statement versus negative statement

Usually people don't respond well to criticisms or complaints. So how can you express these thoughts and feelings without negative responses?

Let's talk about how to get your complaint heard with a positive reaction. Instead of speaking about what you don't like, try expressing what you do like or how you would like things to be. The best way to demonstrate this is with the following examples:

Negative Statement: You look terrible when you walk with your head down.

Positive Statement: You look nice when you have good posture.

> Both statements reflect the same idea. The negative statement would come across as a criticism and probably provoke anger. The positive statement sounds like a compliment, and people don't usually get angry at compliments.

Read the following negative statements and change them to positive.

1. Negative Statement: I hate it when you leave dishes on the counter.
   Positive Statement:

2. Negative Statement: I wish you would use your head once in awhile.
   Positive Statement:

3. Negative Statement: Your room is a mess. You're a slob.
   Positive Statement:

Come up with your own negative statement and change it to positive.

Negative Statement: _____

_____

Positive Statement: _____

_____

improving relationships

1. Write the name of someone you find difficult to interact with.

_____

2. Write what you could do to improve the quality of that relationship.

_____

_____

3. Write what they could do to improve the quality of that relationship.

_____

_____

4. If you are working in a therapeutic setting, ask for feedback. Write any changes you are considering after hearing feedback.

_____

_____

You can continue to problem solve with another relationship here:

1. Write the name of someone you find difficult to interact with. _____

_____

2. Write what you could do to improve the quality of that relationship.

_____

_____

improving relationships practice

3. Write what they could do to improve the quality of that relationship

_____

_____

4. If you are working in a therapeutic setting, ask for feedback. Write any changes you would consider after

hearing feedback.

_____

_____

limited thinking

The following types of thinking distort the truth. This can be bad but sometimes can be used to protect ourselves from negative feelings. It's important to be aware of this thinking.

Overthinking—This happens when someone sees a bad experience and assumes all related experiences will be bad.

Underthinking— This person looks at a situation or problem and makes it appear better than it really is.

Tragedy—This person looks at a problem or situation and magnifies it, making it worse than it really is.

Projecting—This person blames someone or something else for their behavior.

Diverting Attention—This person changes the topic to avoid something that's uncomfortable.

Hostility—This person becomes angry so others will back away.

Withdrawing—This person pulls away or isolates hoping no one will notice them.

Fairytale Thinking—This person thinks nothing bad will ever happen to them; this person feels invincible. This happens often in children and adolescents.

All or Nothing Thinking—This person is either on top of the world or down in the dumps. This person can't protect their ego and has no balance.

Should Have—This person focuses on regrets. He wishes he could turn back time when saying, "I should have ... could have ... would have ..."

Mind Reading—This happens when you assume you know what others are going to say.

when life hands you lemons make lemonade

Directions:

1. Identify the lemons—the negative things in your life—and write them below.
2. If you are in a group, share one of your lemons.
3. Ask the group for feedback on how you can make lemonade, or cope with your situation. If you are alone, you will need to brainstorm on your own.
4. Write down the actions you have decided to take to improve your situation.

_____

_____

_____

_____

_____

_____

_____

_____

_____

_____

_____

_____

To order more copies visit: www.whenlifehandsyoulemonsmakelemonade.com

the perfection monster

If you are living as the Perfection Monster, your goals and standards are set too high. They may never be met which will cause you to feel disappointed.

The following statements reflect unreasonable expectations. Change the unreasonable statements to reasonable. The first one is an example.

Unreasonable statement: I am going to cook a seven-course dinner for the first time to impress my boyfriend.
Reasonable statement: I can make something nice that will make us both happy without going overboard.

Unreasonable Statement: I have to iron all my clothes every day so I will look perfect.

_____

_____

Unreasonable statement: My kids are a reflection of me, so they had better act like angels all the time.

_____

_____

Unreasonable statement: I have to get good grades—straight As.

_____

_____

Unreasonable statement: I have to look perfect for the prom.

_____

_____

Unreasonable statement: I can't let my little brother be better than me.

_____

_____

self-talk

Self-Talk refers to the things we say silently in our heads. The following will explore negative, positive, and neutral kinds of self talk. This activity is particularly helpful if you are suffering from depression.

Negative Self-Talk

Too often we say negative statements in our heads. When we do this we are programing our minds for limitations. If you make a mistake in life, learn from it, and forgive yourself.

Positive Self-Talk

With positive self-talk, we can tell ourselves things like "I am capable," "I can do better," "I will survive," and so forth. Positive thoughts will improve our self-confidence. They allow us to love ourselves and keep our minds healthy. No one will love you more than yourself.

Neutral Self-Talk

Neutral self-talk is not positive or negative. Staying neutral is okay. If you make a mistake and you can't find anything positive to say in your head, try staying neutral. Here's an example: A child forgets to clean her room and feels irresponsible. She could tell herself, *I made a mistake; Simple as that.* Another example: You damaged your husband's car. You could tell yourself, *It was an accident; Accidents happen.*

What kind of neutral or positive self talk would you use to help with the following scenarios?

1. Your parent sent you to your room for eating on the couch. You feel bad.

_____

2. You forgot to feed your neighbor's fish and they died. You feel terrible about it.

_____

3. You talked about someone behind their back and they found out.

_____

4. Your handwriting is sloppy. You feel frustrated.

_____

5. You forgot to attend your friend's birthday party for the second year in a row.

_____

falsely blaming

Blame means to hold someone or something responsible for a fault or wrong.

Sometimes we hold the wrong person responsible for the fault. This happens when we can't cope with reality. For example, a boy was playing on the monkey bars. He let go on purpose and fell to the ground. He landed poorly and broke his ankle. His dad blamed his mom for the broken ankle in order to cope with this horrible accident.

Blaming with Anger:

I was so angry at my sister that I screamed at her and then blamed her for making me do it.

In the future, I need to discuss my feelings of frustration before I explode.

I blamed my twenty-year-old daughter

for being raped by asking, "What were you wearing?"

If the parent doesn't know who the rapist is, he may need to blame the victim to cope with what happened, as twisted as that may be.

In the future he should _____

_____

I blamed my wife

when our child came home with a bad grade by saying, "This bad grade must be your fault!"

In the future I should _____

_____

I blamed my mom

when I got high by saying, "It's your fault because you criticized me."

In the future I should _____

_____

thinking errors quiz

Refer to the Appendix for quiz answers.

1. Codependency is the _____ on a partner who may require support due to illness or addiction.

2. An optimist is someone who thinks _____ about situations.

3. I don't think I can win the contest so I refuse to try. What kind of limited thinking is this?
   _____

4. True or False: Changing a negative statement to a positive one will make people angry.

5. The wife said, "Our friend John looks great. He got his teeth fixed." The husband responded, "Oh, would you rather be with him?" The husband is demonstrating which character flaw?:_____
   _____

6. My hobbies are put aside to participate in your hobbies.
   This is _____ behavior.

7. When you uncover automatic negative thoughts it's important to change them to _____
   _____ .

8. If your glass of water is at the ½ way mark, and you are not happy nor sad then you think like a
   a. pessimist
   b. realist
   c. optimist

part 3:
fix my family

family functioning

Parents need to agree on how to raise their children. When the parents don't agree, the children get confused. They may play one parent against the other or take sides. This will create controversy between the parents which will create an additional problem. I encourage parents to compromise. This way they can stand united and support each other.

Here's an example of a family that was having difficulties.
The father was viewed by the mother as too strict. The mother was viewed by the father as too lenient. The child sided with the mother, causing the dad to feel like the bad guy. Both parents wanted to see their son do the right thing and stay out of trouble. What advice would you give them?
What are some skills from this book that can help this family? _____

_____

_____

_____

_____

_____

_____

_____

_____

_____

_____

_____

family dynamics

If you draw a triangle to represent a family of three, it might look like this:

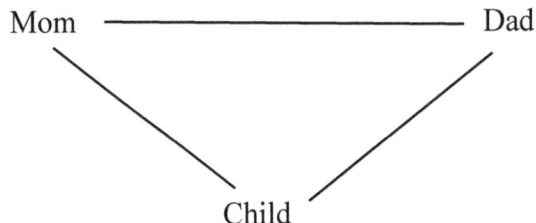

```
   Mom ————————————— Dad
       \           /
        \         /
         \       /
          Child
```

This shows that the mom and dad are at the head of the family and the child obeys rules and follows the structure set by the parents.

How would you describe this relationship?

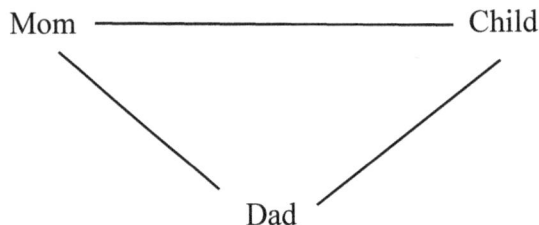

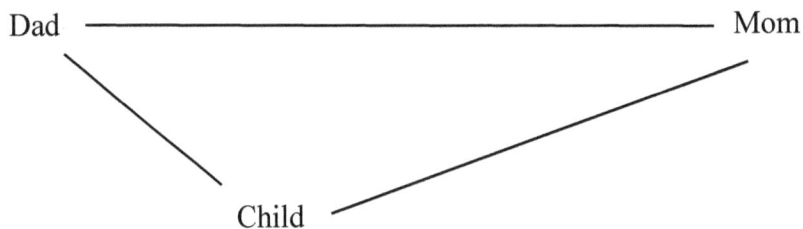

```
   Mom ————————————— Child
       \           /
        \         /
         \       /
           Dad
```

This shows that the mom and child are in control of the family and dad's opinion holds no weight.

How would you describe this relationship?

```
   Dad ——————————————————— Mom
       \                 /
        \              /
         \           /
          Child ——
```

Both parents are at the top but notice that the child is closer to dad. One reason for this could be that the child has an alignment with dad, or the mom works many hours.

How would this family's triangle look? The father works many hours. The mother is an alcoholic. The fourteen-year-old son takes care of his mother. On one occasion, he had to steer the car to get them home.

This story continues as the mom gets help and becomes sober. The son, however, has difficulty letting go of the responsibility he had acquired. Hence, he goes to counseling. During counseling, he decides to try to be a 14 year old kid again.

Each family member should draw his or her own picture of what their family looks like. If you do not have a family of three, draw a tree with branches. The top of the tree will represent the authority figures and the other branches can extend as far or as close as you want to represent each relationship. Afterwards, discuss your trees with each other.

Does your family agree on one view? Is that view a healthy one?
Write what steps each member can take to improve the functioning of your family. _____

_____

_____

_____

_____

_____

_____

children's roles in the family

Sometimes parents cast their children into roles. These roles can maintain a sense of balance for the family if they are done lightheartedly, or they can be harmful if the children are pigeonholed into them.

The Flawless Child —This child has to be perfect so the family can brag about him. This child takes the focus off of the family's dysfunction. The Flawless Child has a lot of pressure to maintain his status for the family.

The Troublemaker—The Troublemaker draws attention away from the family's dysfunction by creating a new problem. The family is focused on the Troublemaker's behavior and does not resolve their other conflicts.

The Disappearing Artist—The Disappearing Artist disappears from the dysfunction of the family. He spends his time in his room, listening to music with earphones. The Disappearing Artist does not want to place any additional demands on the family. The consequences he experiences are becoming uncomfortable when conflicts arise.

Mom's Little Friend or Dad's Little Friend—This implies that the parents, as a couple, are too dysfunctional to fix their own problems so each confide in their child. The child may feel responsible to help but will have difficulty processing adult problems. The child will likely experience feelings of discomfort and frustration.

The Parentified Child—This child is given too much responsibility which leads to control in the family. She is now acting like a parent. This child misses out on being a kid.

The Helpful Child— The family brags about how helpful this child is but in reality he is treated like a servant. He is expected to take care of the whole family. This child is often responsible for the care of younger siblings. This child rarely gets to enjoy her childhood.

It is possible to identify with more than one role. An only child may identify with all of these roles at one time or another. If you feel you are stuck in a role, point this out to your family. If you are a parent who has cast their child into a role, you should point this out to your family as well.

family exercise:

Draw a symbolic picture of how your family looks to you now. Each family member should make their own picture. If the client would like to draw his or her picture in this workbook, they should do so below.

Here is an example of a symbolic picture of a dysfunctional family:

In this picture the Dad and Mom are first, meaning they are the authority figures in the family. The Dad is near City Hall because of the saying, "You can't fight City Hall." This means that Dad was always right or always got his way. This was frustrating to the three females, thus the reason for the split. The Mom and the two children went on outings without the Dad, since he never wanted to go anyway.

Draw your picture here:

Family Exercise: After you all have drawn your pictures, explain them to your family. Family members are to listen without interrupting. Next, a discussion should occur using clarifying statements; *so what you're saying is…* Everyone may have a different view, and all views should be considered.

Finally, each individual should come up with at least three things that they could do differently to promote a healthier family. Record everyone's suggestions here.

_____

_____

_____

parenting

If you usually use punishment as your form of discipline, it can result in some children wanting revenge and others experiencing feelings of no self-worth. You may want to try giving your child a chance to make amends as a form of discipline.

Let's explore some outcomes of punishment:

Feeling vengeful:

1. I'll do it again, but next time I won't get caught.

2. I'll break some other rule to get back at them, but this time I won't get caught.

3. I will run away from home. That will hurt them.

Feeling bad:

1. How could I be so stupid?

2. I don't deserve _____.

3. I will punish myself for making that mistake.

4. How could my parents love such a rotten kid?

Physical punishment (spanking):

1. My parent lost control and spanked me. I hate him or her.

2. My parents say that hitting is wrong so why did they hit me?

3. My parent lost control and hit me. They don't allow me to loose control.

4. My parent shows that he/she has control over my body.

Feeling powerless:

1. I have no control over my room because you say it's your house.

2. I have no control over my body. You seem to own that too, by spanking me.

3. I am never offered the chance to correct my mistakes.

4. I need control over something so I might use drugs, cut myself, tattoo my body, choose to look freakish, or engage in risky behavior.

Making amends and negotiating is on page 49

making amends and negotiating

1. Making amends means to compensate or make up for a wrongdoing.

   Parent: You broke the neighbor's window with your baseball. What can you do to fix the problem?

   Child's Response: I can do jobs around the house to earn money to pay for the new window.

2. Negotiating means to discuss and reach an agreement.

   Parent: You did not clean your room as you were told. Now you will lose computer time.

   Child: Can I clean my room, rake the yard, and do some laundry instead?

3. Summarize means to give a brief statement of the main points.

   Along with your child fixing the problem, discuss together how he or she could make better choices in the future.

4. Wrap up: Lastly, let your child know that you do not like what they did, but you still love them. This will promote a healthy self-esteem and is important with any form of discipline.

overcoming power struggles

Power struggles can happen in any relationship such as married couples, siblings, friends...
The skills below will help in any relationship.

Clarify: As someone speaks to you, repeat what they said, or translate in your own words. Example: "So what you're saying is..."

Negotiate: Sometimes things seem unfair, so negotiating a compromise may be an option. Example: "It seems unfair for you to make me stay in the house for a month. What can I do to regain your trust?

***I* statements versus *You* statements:**
Using the word *I* is friendly and invites cooperation. It's helpful to start sentences with "*I* feel ..."
Using the word *You* is confrontational. It can be viewed as an attack before you finish your sentence and most likely will cause an argument. Please note that saying, "*I feel that you* ..." This would be a *You statement.*

Feeling Words: Feeling words are words that express emotions. These are words like *frustrated, disrespected, powerless, appreciated, proud,* and *happy.* These words help others understand you better and help you to stay healthy.

If you are working in a group or with a therapist, try role--playing a scenario using these skills.

fix my family quiz

Refer to the Appendix for quiz answers.

1. True/False: It's healthy for parents to establish roles for their children.

2. True/False: It's okay for parents to disagree on their rules because the child will listen to one of them.

3. All family members should learn and use the skills in this book to

   obtain a _____ family.

4. Punishment can create feelings of _____ or feeling _____ about oneself.

5. Making amends means to _____ your wrongdoing.

   "Negotiating" means to discuss a _____.

6. When overcoming power struggles, it is important to use

   A. clarifying statements

   B. punishment

   C. negotiation

   D. A and C

7. A statement that begins with the word *you* can be viewed as _____.

8. Feeling words will help others _____ you.

9. It's common for parents and their children to have _____ struggles.

part 4:
recovery

identifying if you have a problem

Do you have a problem with drugs or alcohol?
Circle all the bullets that apply to you.

1. Preoccupation is being distracted with the thought of something else.
   - You look forward to a treat at the end of the day.
   - You look forward to the end of the week "party" that starts on Thursday.
   - You like your personality under the influence.

2. Gulping your drinks or using drugs quickly
   - You order a double or do shots
   - You have a couple of drinks or smoke some marijuana before going to the party

3. Increased tolerance
   - You can drink or use drugs more than others and not show the effects.
   - You drive a car because you think you are fine.
   - You wonder about your increased ability to handle more. You are sometimes proud of it and sometimes scared of it.

4. Using alcohol or drugs as medicine
   - You continue using to avoid withdrawl.
   - You take one drug to overcome the effects of another.
   - You have a drink to alleviate your stressful day.
   - You drink or smoke marijuana to calm your nerves.
   - You drink at social events to feel more comfortable.
   - You use alcohol or drugs to help you sleep.
   - You use alcohol or drugs to alleviate pain.

5. Using alone
   - You have used drugs when no one was around.
   - You stopped at a bar by yourself.

6. Blackouts
   - You can't remember what took place the night before.
   - You have no idea how you got home.

7. Hidden supply
   - You have hidden a stash of alcohol/drugs in your house.
   - You have hidden a stash in your car.

identifying if you have a problem part 2

8. Consequences
- You have been charged with DUI/DWI.
- Family and friends have distanced themselves.
- Your physical health is declining.
- You have been admitted into a rehabilitation facility.
- Your job has suffered or school grades have gone down.
- You have experienced an overdose.
- You have put the purchase of drugs/alcohol before your financial responsibilities.

9. Behavioral changes
- When intoxicated, you act in a foolish or nasty manner.
- You stole money to buy drugs/alcohol.
- You substitute one drug for another, thinking that avoiding certain drugs will make you sane.
- You avoid certain people that would not approve of your drug use.

10. Emotional struggles
- You have felt guilty or ashamed about your actions and then became defensive.
- Using drugs is making your home life unhappy.
- The thought of running out of your substance of choice terrifies you.
- You are beginning to experience psychiatric symptoms like depression, paranoia, mania, panic attacks, or suicidal thinking.

identifying stressors in your life

1. I feel resentful when_____

_____

2. I feel lost when_____

_____

3. I feel scared when_____

_____

4. I feel sad when _____

_____

5. I feel bad when _____

_____

6. I feel disappointed when_____

_____

7. I feel hatred when _____

_____

8. I feel frustrated when _____

_____

9. I feel overwhelmed when _____

_____

10. I feel anxious when _____

_____

who am i?

Use the word list or come up with your own ideas to answer the questions below.

word list

cute	happy	playful	fearless	grateful	sad
attention-seeking	rivals	brave	strange	silly	smart
argumentative	cooperative	insecure	goofy	quiet	honest
talkative	different	creative	hopeful	inspired	dumb
curious	outgoing	stubborn	sneaky	honest	dishonest
loving	patient	scared	demanding	popular	

Describe your personality when you were a child.

_____

_____

_____

Describe your personality now.

_____

_____

_____

Describe the person you want to be.

_____

_____

_____

behavior

How are you powerless over your use of drugs/alcohol? Complete the following questions.

The loved ones I have hurt: _____

_____

_____

The friends I have lost: _____

_____

_____

The money I have spent: _____

_____

_____

The personal items I have traded or sold: _____

_____

_____

The places/people I have stole from: _____

_____

_____

The lies I have told others and myself: _____

_____

_____

ten excuses against sobriety

1. I can handle it. It isn't a problem yet.

2. I only have to avoid my drug of choice.

3. I have to attend holiday parties and special occasions?

4. I'm not giving up my friends. They won't use around me.

5. I lost my license and have no way of getting to a meeting.

6. At meetings they will ask my sobriety date and I don't want to tell.

7. I can go to bars for the food and music.

8. Just because I lost my license doesn't mean I have a problem.

9. What will I do for fun?

10. I don't like myself or my life when I am sober.

exploring gains

You may have several reasons for using mind-altering chemicals. Think about these reasons and categorize them into primary and secondary gains.

Primary gains describe your top reasons for using drugs.
Secondary gains describe a gain that's not so obvious. It could be to manipulate your parents, gain someone's attention, or cry out for help.

Write your gains below. Next to each gain put a #1 for primary and a #2 for secondary: _____

_____

_____

_____

_____

_____

_____

_____

_____

Once you are aware of your motivation for using chemicals, try to come up with a solution. If you use drugs because your parents frustrate you, try talking to them about your frustration. You could also seek help from

a therapist. Write some alternative ways to handle your circumstances. _____

_____

_____

_____

_____

_____

relapse

The following are symptoms that may cause relapse. Rank each symptom from 1 to 8. 1 is most threatening and 8 is least threatening *to you*.

(___) Boredom—There's not enough activity in my life, so my mind thinks about drugs.

(___) Lies—I begin with telling small lies to others and eventually start lying to myself.

(___) Impatient feeling —I have too much idle time. Things are not happening fast enough.

(___) Argumentative—Since I can't use I am going to argue ridiculous points of view until I create an excuse to use.

(___) Depression—Sadness can occur now that you are clean/sober. This could create an excuse to use.

(___) Frustration—I want things to go my way, and when they don't, I want to use.

(___) Overconfident—Now that I am clean, I no longer fear addiction.

(___) Feather-brained thinking—Now that I have achieved some clean time, I will stay away from my drug of choice and use an alternative drug with no problem.

letter from your enemy

Hello, My Friend,

I've missed you since our last encounter, but knew you would visit me once again. I am pleased to be the first thing you wake up to and the last thing you touch before you go to bed or blackout. I appreciate that you wake up all hours of the night, with chills and sweats. It amuses me to watch you hug the toilet, heaving and retching, unable to keep me down. It's wonderful to see how much destruction I can do to your liver while at the same time destroying your brain bit by bit. Only a true friend like you would sacrifice so much for me. I could kill you, but I'll be happy to keep you sick, put you in the hospital, or another rehab. You know I'll be waiting for you when you get out.

I love the effect I have on you mentally, when you can't think straight; physically, as you lack coordination; and socially, as you're all alone because no one will tolerate your crazy behavior—how I love that crazy behavior! I enjoy making you restless so you can never relax and irritabile so everything and everybody makes you uncomfortable. I love it when you become so confused that you can't make a simple decision. I want to make you *hate* everything, especially yourself. Lol. I'll help you feel guilt and remorse for the things you have done for I know you won't be able to let them go. I promise to make you fearful and paranoid for no reason at all. I will drive you slowly insane as I put your mind, body, and soul in living *hell!*

I thank you for the countless good jobs you've lost for me. The fine friends you deeply cared for, you gave up for me. And what about your family? The most important people in the world, you threw them all away all for me. I cannot express the gratitude I feel for your loyalty. You sacrificed all these beautiful things in life just to devote yourself to me. But do not despair, my friend, for you can always depend on me.

Sincerely yours,
Alcohol and Drugs

reality in recovery

Does relapse erase all recovery progress up to that point?

A brief relapse will temporarily stop recovery, but the skills you have learned for staying safe and clean are still with you. Pick yourself up, determine where you went wrong, and make some changes.

Is relapse inevitable?

Relapse is not inevitable. Take one day at a time and watch for symptoms such as boredom, lying, and depression. Refer to page 62 for more information.

Is recovery the same as abstinence?

No. You can abstain from drug use for a temporary period of time, perhaps to pass a drug test, but that does not mean you are in recovery. Recovery is working toward a healthy state of mind.

Will triggers remain forever?

Triggers may be extinguished over time. As you become healthier they may not be so tempting.

Can I achieve recovery alone?

Perhaps, but a support group, healthy friends and family can be important with accountability and encouragement.

change your future

To achieve a healthy recovery you need to change negative situations in your life. Fill out the following.

People who are toxic to my recovery and why.

_____

_____

Places that are toxic to my recovery and why.

_____

_____

Things I see that are toxic to my recovery and why.

_____

_____

Feelings I have that toxic to my recovery and why. Example: Hatred

_____

_____

Considering all of the above, which do you think will be the most challenging to change in your recovery?

_____

_____

I plan to seek assistance from_____by_____

_____

_____

resulting behavior

Since addictive behavior hurts others, how can you make amends?

I have hurt _____

by_____
_____

I plan to make things right by

_____
_____

I have hurt _____

by_____
_____

I plan to make things right by

_____
_____

I have hurt _____

by_____
_____

I plan to make things right by

_____
_____

The people you have hurt may not forgive you, and that is their right. You still have to take ownership of your wrong doings.

harboring a secret game

1. Write any secrets you have on a piece of paper; one secret per paper. If you don't have a secret write a hypothetical situations that would be relevant to recovery.
2. Place all the secrets in a bag.
3. Pull out a secret and read it. The group should offer helpful suggestions on how to handle each secret.

moderation

The negative consequences to getting high will outweigh the positive. Can you think of alternative activities you would enjoy that would be safe from harm and clean from substances?

_____

_____

_____

_____

_____

_____

Doing anything in excess is not healthy. Moderation is the way to go.

Make a list of positive things that you want to happen as a result of discontinuing drug use.

_____

_____

_____

_____

_____

_____

don't forget!

Remember where you have been …

Have you ever had a sprained ankle or broken arm? Until it healed, it was probably difficult to do certain things. After it healed, you may have forgotten about the difficulties you encountered.

Once you have stopped using mind-altering chemicals and are on the right track to recovery, you may forget the struggles you have been through. This could lead to relapse.

Come up with a plan to prevent relapse. Try to be specific. Here are five suggestions that you can elaborate on.

1. Attend twelve-step meetings.
2. Seek help if you need it by...
3. Accept your past.
4. Stay healthy by...
5. Use the skills you have learned such as...

_____

_____

_____

_____

_____

_____

_____

_____

_____

substance recovery exit plan

Instructions: Check all the entries that you can and will do. Please do not check something that you have no intention of doing. Be honest with yourself.

_____I will attend twelve-step meetings sponsored by NA or AA _____ times per week.

_____I will communicate my feelings without blaming people, places, or things.

_____I will accept responsibility for things I have done wrong.

_____I will try to make amends for things I have done wrong.

_____I will continue to interact with my sponsor.

_____I plan to complete the 12 steps from NA/AA programs.

_____I will continue to interact with healthy people, places, and things.

_____I will identify old patterns of behavior and work to change them.

_____I will engage in the following healthy activities:

_____

_____

_____

_____

_____I will seek help from my higher power.

_____I believe that continuing my efforts toward recovery is the right thing to do.

_____I will focus on one day at a time.

Print name:_____

Signature:_____

Date:_____

recovery quiz

Refer to the Appendix for quiz answers.

1. Yes/No Recovery is the same as abstinence.

2. I can get overwhelmed if I don't take _____ at a time.

3. Yes/No Relapse is inevitable.

4. Any activity I do should be in _____.

5. "I can handle my drug use" is an _____ to continue using.

6. True/False: If I avoid my drug of choice, I will no longer have a problem.

7. True /False: I don't need to give up my friends because they promised not to use around me.

8. Self-pity, boredom, and telling lies may cause _____.

9. Addictive behavior often _____ others.

10. Using alone, an increased tolerance, and hiding your supply are symptoms that you have a _____

    _____.

measuring success chart in a rehabilitation program

Objective: The client will achieve 4 out of 5 boxes a day and must stay safe from harm and clean from substances to complete this therapeutic program. (Length of stay may vary.)

	Mon	Tues	Wed	Thurs	Fri
Safe from harm and clean from substances					
Skills used at home					
Skills used in the program					
Daily goal achieved					
Teach a family member or friend a new skill					

Safe refers to avoiding certain people, places, and things that are unhealthy to your well-being. **Clean** refers to staying drug-free and alcohol-free, not harming yourself (including tattoos, piercings, and body mutilation), and not harming others.

Skills used at home refers to using skill that you have learned in this program at home.

Skills used in the program refers to using a skill you have learned with peers and counselors.

Daily goal means that you select a short-term goal for the day. It could be to learn something new or discuss something that's troubling you.

Teach a family member or friend a new skill refers to choosing a skill you learned and explaining it to someone outside of the program. Both parties are expected to use this new skill.

Note: If you are in an inpatient setting, you will need to delete the "Skills used at home" box. If you meet with a counselor or therapist for fewer than five days a week, you will need to use fewer boxes.

The author gives permission for the reader to photocopy and use the "Measuring Success Chart in a Rehabilitation Program".

appendix

quiz answers

Help Me Cope:	1. False; 2. True; 3. False; 4. C; 5. Exercise; 6. Hurt; 7. A; 8. C; 9. Use feeling words, positive self talk, teach my family the skills in this book; 10. Positive
Thinking Errors:	1. Reliance; 2. Positively; 3. All or Nothing; 4 False; 5. Overly-sensitive; 6. Codependent; 7. Positive; 8. Realist
Fix My Family:	1. False; 2. False; 3. Healthy; 4. Revenge, bad; 5. Compensate or make up for, Compromise; 6. D; 7. Confrontational; 8. Understand; 9. Power
Recovery:	1. No; 2. One day; 3. No; 4. Moderation; 5. Excuse; 6. False; 7. False; 8. Relapse; 9. Hurts; 10. Problem

WHEN LIFE HANDS YOU LEMONS, MAKE LEMON-AIDE

helpful sites and suggested reading

911
If you're facing a life threatening emergency or dangerous situation, call 911.

National Suicide Prevention Lifeline
(800) 273-8255

The National Domestic Violence Hotline
(800) 799-safe (7233)
Hearing impaired (800) 787-3224 (TTY)

APS National Adult Protective Services
(202) 370-6292

Narcotics Anonymous
www.na.org

Alcoholics Anonymous
www.aa.org

"How to Talk So Kids Will Listen and Listen So Kids Will Talk,"
by Adele Faber and Elaine Mazlish, www.faber/mazlish

"Men are from Mars and Women are from Venus,"
by John Gray

To order more copies visit: www.whenlifehandsyoulemonsmakelemonade.com

bibliography

Schultz, Duane *Theories of Personality, Third Edition* (Monterey, California: Brooks/Cole Publishing Company, A Division of Wadsworth, Inc. 1986, 1981, 1976

Bowen, Murray MD "Eight Concepts, Triangles"
www.thebowencenter.org

Jantz, Gregory L. PhD "The Power of Positive Self-Talk"
www.psychologytoday.com/us/flag/hope-relationships/201605/the-power-of-positive-self-talk/

Burns, David MD "The Top 10 Types of 'Stinkin Thinking'"
www.feelinggood.com

Maslow, Abraham PhD "Maslow's Hierarchy of Need"
www.simplypsychology.org/maslow/

Kubler Ross, Elisabeth and Kessler, David "The 5 Stages of Grief"
www.grief.com/the-five-stages-of-grief/

McKay, Matthew; Davis, Martha; and Fanning, Patrick "Thoughts and Feelings Summary"
www.blog.12min.com

Faber, Adele and Mazlish, Elaine *How To Talk So Kids WIll Listen and Listen So Kids Will Talk* www.faber/mazlish

www.ingramcontent.com/pod-product-compliance
Lightning Source LLC
Chambersburg PA
CBHW080254030426

42334CB00023BA/2813